EXIT OPERA

EXIT OPERA

Poems

KIM ADDONIZIO

W. W. NORTON & COMPANY

Independent Publishers Since 1923

For information about permission to reproduce selections from this book, write to
Permissions, W. W. Norton & Company, Inc., 500 Fifth Avenue, New York, NY 10110

For information about special discounts for bulk purchases, please contact
W. W. Norton Special Sales at specialsales@wwnorton.com or 800-233-4830

Manufacturing by Versa Press
Production manager: Devon Zahn

ISBN 978-1-324-07893-7

W. W. Norton & Company, Inc., 500 Fifth Avenue, New York, N.Y. 10110
www.wwnorton.com

W. W. Norton & Company Ltd., 15 Carlisle Street, London W1D 3BS

1 2 3 4 5 6 7 8 9 0

For Danny,

making beauty.

In dark times
Will there also be singing?
Yes, there will be singing.
About the dark times.
—BERTOLT BRECHT

Fasten your seatbelts.
It's going to be a bumpy night.
—BETTE DAVIS IN *ALL ABOUT EVE*

Contents

II

III

Exit Opera

The shieldmaiden waits in the wings. The operagoers wait, shifting in
    their seats.
Out in the forest the ember waits in its cigarette to make its black mark on
    the world,

not content to ravage a few rolled tobacco leaves. It wants to show
it can murder more trees than the last bitter fire. In the sequoia grove,

in record heat, tourists wait for a chance to stand inside an enormous
    burn-hollowed tree
while the bark waits the years it takes to grow over the scar. Legions of
    charred trees,

legions of kids clambering over rocks. In the troposphere, the next giant
    pyrocumulonimbus cloud
waits to be born from its gassy parents. Once the opera's begun,

you must wait for what feels like eons for Brünnhilde to deliver her aria as
    she throws herself
on the funeral pyre & everyone goes up in flames. Once you escape a
    wildfire,

leaving everything behind, a little void appears beneath your heart &

    lodges in your ribs.

Again you must wait. If you see lightning, listen for the thunder to tell you

    how far

or near you are. When Milton went blind, he felt useless, but then he

    decided it was okay

to stand still. To abide. Look at the trees, who are patient, who suffer us to

    touch them.

EXISTENTIAL VOYAGE

Maybe you'll understand this life when you slam
your fist into a cloud. When you're lashed to the mast
listening to the songs of space aliens
trying to dash you on the rocks of hermeneutic texts.
But probably not. Let's eat too much and drink
our faces off; anything else is a waste of time
although time is also hard to understand,
maybe made of quantum bits but maybe not,
flowing or passing, maybe an arrow, maybe
a total delusion like believing in griffins
or lasting justice for the poor.
Parmenides and Heraclitus forever at war
about the nature of reality. Are tensed facts
or tenseless facts ontologically fundamental?
I don't get it, either. More tequila? Hold this lime
while I pour salt into my navel.
Lick, shoot, suck. Quark, lepton, boson.
Teeny-tiny invisible neutrinos.
At least the ancient Greek gods
let us see them occasionally. I don't see
how anyone can cleat-hitch their life to prayer.

Who do you think is listening—

maybe a great glowing abyssopelagic snail

or the single resident of Monowi, Nebraska.

So how, wondered the lonely philosopher,

counteract the omnipresent nil?

Camus suggested suicide was rational,

but to exit thus is to forever have slain

the hearts of those you've left behind.

Better to enlist in the employ of snowmelt

or slime yourself to a sepal,

transmute the base metals of your anxieties

into a giant rose-gold sestina. To remember

that neither despair nor a dearth of taxis can last.

When the cargo shifts, the boat may list,

requiring heavy lifting before it can be righted.

When you lose sight of the shore,

the sea will take you where you need to go.

20.5 LIGHT YEARS FROM EARTH

Sometimes writing feels so stupid I think I should get out into the world &
   do something
like repairing fountain pens, milking snakes, something useful—

sexing chickens, dyeing lemons—fecal pathobiologist is another job I
   could maybe do
if only I would slide off my couch & stop reading & writing so much.

Some days it feels like everything is stupid, like when I'm feeling
   existentially nihilistic
& reading Tolstoy who saw four answers to the basic question of *What's the*
   point:

1. Just be ignorant
2. Be an Epicurean, "disregarding the dragon and the mice, & licking the
   honey in the best way"
3. Go ahead & kill yourself (the strong way)
4. (the weak Tolstoy way) "knowing that life is a stupid joke played upon
   us, and still to go on living, washing oneself, dressing, dining,
   talking, & even writing books"

Drugs are stupid but I like them anyway, how they build a little cellar
to shelter me from the tornadoes of my bad thoughts & feelings.

Stupid, my brother used to call me, & *Stupid*, I call myself when I lose my keys
or my entire car or stagger too much.
Drunkenness is stupid but see drugs, above.

Exoplanet hunting: probably too much math required to find any
    habitable planets.
There is a 10–20 percent likelihood that we are not alone, but so what?

Billions of people right here on earth & a lot of them are lonely,
sobbing into takeout cartons of soba noodles.

Hallucinating in Solitary.
Getting diapered in Assisted Living.

Tolstoy finally came to a kind of acceptance after thinking about reason vs.
    faith
& some hooey about how content the peasants were.

It's best to be stupidly mad for someone, as in
I am insanely in love with you does not mean
Please medicate me before I put my fist through the folding glass door of a bus

or get naked & wave my underwear on the roof to signal the visitors from Gliese 581g,

the sixth & possibly habitable planet orbiting the red dwarf Gliese 581.

Alligator wrangler.

Train pusher.

Crime scene cleaner.

Dulce et utile is the life of the pig wanker.

Today I saw a Greenpeace worker in front of Starbucks holding a clipboard,

    repeating

Take a minute to save the earth? Stupid me, I went for ice cream.

SOME OF THE QUESTIONS TO CONSIDER

Is it better to offer your heart to the wolf

or wait for the wolf to tear it out of you?

It's hard to know which is worse,

the nightmare of approaching tornadoes

or waking from the dream your parents were alive in.

Enter the ominous music announcing the shark.

It is best to disappear into one's work.

Best to be ceaselessly drunk, Baudelaire suggested,

mentioning other things besides wine but most people

ignored that part, because who wants to be drunk on virtue?

Misreadings are best. Misunderstandings are also best

but to be misunderstood is not the goal.

I don't need drugs, I am drugs, Dalí famously said,

and drew his wife's face exploding into spheres.

What do all these wildflowers mean? *Just look*,

said a famous American painter who, drunk, drove his convertible

off the road into the trees and flew headfirst into an oak.

We're all afloat in the same solution.

Would you like to trade some molecules with me?

Better to sketch a few atoms than fire neutrons at them

to create a chain reaction. The adult human body contains

seven octillion atoms and one picnic table. Is it time to go?

Not yet, not yet. Let's meet for an aperitivo.

Let's build a pineapple from all this fresh snow.

MY OPERA

takes place in a dive bar, it's all drunken recitative,

okay maybe an aria sung by a feral kitten, one

by a skittish donkey, maybe one without words

just the sounds of lovemaking, moans, laughter, wailing,

it ends with a dramatic flourish like smashing a glass

in the fireplace, I always wanted to do that

& watch the flames flare up. It's not a long opera,

maybe fourscore years give or take, everyone

gets their own glass & pours out whatever's in it

onto the floor. The staging is difficult. Exploding stars

are involved, high-redshift galaxies, interior chambers,

a little country blues, a little jazz guitar, a jam jar containing

a tiny ocean & a tinier rowboat rocking gently in the swells

that I am steering toward you in the dark.

GAMES PEOPLE PLAY

You be the dissatisfied master and I'll be the naughty maid.

You be the Roman centurion; I'll be the sorrowful, impaled savior of
humankind.

You be a plague of locusts. I'll be sledding in the Arctic circle.

You're the last human alive and I'm a horde of zombies lurching toward
your house; run!

I'm right and you're locked in the basement.

You be an abortion. I'll be such a baby.

I'll be a beautiful statue that won't come to life. You'll be, like, *Perfect*.

You be Higher Consciousness; I'll just be high.

I'm an air conditioner in a heat wave, and you're a blacked-out
electrical grid.

I'm a global pandemic and you're a right-wing radiologist who knows
nothing about epidemiology.

I'm a conspiracy theorist and you're impersonating a crisis actor.

You be the chandelier crashing down in the ballroom. I'll be the legs
sticking out beneath it.

I am the food of love; eat your heart out.

I've got a magic cloak and you've got an MBA.

You're my soulmate, and I am Marie of Roumania.

You're Marie of Roumania and I'm Dorothy Parker.

I'm the Watts Towers and you're a communist housing block.

You be the renowned research scientist. I'll be caged and pulling the lever
for banana pellets.

You be a dead language; I'll be an extinct civilization.

Maybe you could just be dead. I'll be the sound of the lid banging down.

SELF-PORTRAIT AS A GOLDFISH TRAPPED IN A TOILET

To be stuck at reception with a man who fucked you once: another
    opportunity
to feel like a small freshwater fish

& remember those nights back in the Precambrian, before you'd evolved
from a primitive life form that would gulp some whiskey at a party

& then float off in a stranger's car to a bed above a garage
& lie there spinelessly for the zeptoseconds it took him

Back then there was hardly any oxygen & no one was woke
Orgasms with men were a few billion years away

Orgasms: You had no idea how to get one
Men: dining & dashing while you were still pulling out your chair

He's married now, he's got kids, good for him
Another opportunity for revenge fantasies:

Shadowy wraiths drag him from the hotel ballroom
down through the gates of Dis, where there's no open bar

A fetal alien creature long dormant in a cheese puff

slithers down his throat, bursts from his stomach & races under a long

    white tablecloth

You could follow it & hide under there until everyone leaves

But he's the first to turn away & it's just like before

He's done & moving away from you in record time

Time: what you wasted being even briefly attracted to people like him

You: flushed out to sea once more

INSOMNIA SONG

Life, friends, is boring. We must not say so. —Berryman

Life, friends, is terrifying . . . we must not say so
Yet here I am . . . & I'm not the only one . . .

Some people like a pink cloud . . . to float themselves & their friends
past a velvet cord & into an exclusive club . . . with no windows . . .

I like to see a woman lurching down a trash-filled sidewalk, chugging an
　　airline bottle of vodka
& tossing it at my feet . . .

I like a person who sees clearly, & can't handle it . . . who wants a
　　thunder shirt
like the ones that calm dogs, just to get through the day . . .

Some people hear the songs of redwoods, & transcribe them in
　　motivational lyrics
employing faulty grammar & banal phraseology . . .

My people lie awake at night, waiting for a giant, shallow-rooted tree
or a hunk of space debris to fall on them . . . ruminating . . . on subduction
　　& sonic attacks

Black thought-balloons bumping along the ceiling, decanting
   microbial demons
that lean down & carefully insert needles of dread along our meridians

Our hearts . . . decelerating . . . to a dirge . . . no one wants to hear
because my people . . . are a drag . . . like this poem . . .

You should stop reading now . . . Go tear off someone's petals
& fall upon the memory foam of life, instead of lying there

like a fossil entombed in a rock, wondering how much time is left
as you listen to the faraway sounds of migratory birds

falling dead into arroyos . . . *thump, thump, thump, thump, thump,*
thump, thump, thump . . . a spiny lobster scraping its way

over bleached brain coral . . . Go be happy . . . *thump, thump, thump* . . .
I prefer to stay here . . . saying many pointless things . . . to no one

& in that way go on . . . not killing myself . . . or anyone else
like an ugly flower

in an impenetrable forest, where no prince will come along
to ruin everything . . .

SWOON

I'm seeing the boulder rolled away. I'm filling with ichor
& holy Sliquid, lubed up like a spaceship, what planet are you from?
Come lick my wounds. My winding sheet's in shreds
in the dirt. Little scraps fluttering up like white-petaled birds
& other nonsense. *Fool for you:* no; idiot: no; jaguar
blitzed on hallucinogenic caapi roots
or capuchin on a millipede maybe & yes I painted my cave
to make it ready for the next thousand centuries of you.

Lunacy! Piracy! Breathe on me & I'm done for!
Noli me tangere, my prehistoric horses will dissolve.
What about that turtle we saw in the cemetery,
will it ever make it back to the lake? Should we have helped it,
lifted it shell & all? How did you get here, anyway—
stirring me like a photovoltaic martini. How classic. How recklessly cliché.

GETTING TO KNOW YOU

I like crawling into a refrigerator & emerging into a space station, how
    about you?
I like a Harry Warren tune sung by Marianne Faithfull, it sounds like the
    Weimar Republic without Germans,

no offence to Germans, that's just my trigger word, a wormhole to a galaxy
of historical trauma, at least a hundred billion galaxies in the universe

& that's a lot of marbles in the jar plus the jar keeps expanding & how many
galaxies of pain, how many of grabbing the person next to you

because whichever all-inclusive nightmare has ended for a New York
    minute & everyone's
weeping & marrying like drunken rabbits?

I love a destination wedding I can't afford, how about we have one
in storm-flooded London, Wellies for everyone

& is Venice still sinking, I like a gondolier, how about Paris in July at 106
    degrees,
Da, da, da, da, da, da, da

Terra Chips, Netflix & opiates, how about you?

Did you know the Crab Nebula glows blue, what a little satellite can do

until the lights go out & all the candles collapse

& stutter how how how

I wish I could leave this planet with you.

IN ASSISI

This souvenir shop is full of skinny wooden crucified Christs
like there weren't enough of those in the churches already

I guess everyone has to believe in something
Crystals, colonics, when you die you get virgins or your very own planet
where you can spin for eternity in your celestial underpants

Some people believe Jesus spoke to Saint Francis, but I have a feeling
Jesus is just going to hang there silently
looking holy & tormented for another two thousand years or so

I don't think I'm going to get a Catholic miracle, like a statue blinks at me
& I suddenly understand Italian Greek Latin Aramaic & Ugaritic

or peel off my tattoos & send the carved lions of my higher self
to tear apart the lambs of my addictions

I'll probably just go on kneeling before minibars in hotel rooms
in my silk robe of flowers, praising the macadamias

One story about Saint Francis is that two years before he died he got stigmata
Probably malaria or leprosy, but imagine those sores

He dressed in a mended sack & old worn sandals

If you saw him in Berkeley you might cross the street to avoid him

then come back with some change & try not to touch his hand

At the end of his life he was going blind, living in a reed hut overrun

    by mice

Mice slithering over his feet, mice climbing the table to sit on his plate

I guess they figured out that the job of a saint is to suffer as horribly as

    possible

Joan of Arc burned & cast into the Seine

Saint Agnes raped & stabbed in the throat

Oliver Plunkett:

imprisoned

hanged

drawn & quartered

beheaded

beatified

canonized

Brother Sun, Sister-in-Law Death, forgive me

I don't see the point of all this pain, or believing it gets better

when you're boxed & delivered to the parade of microbes that will devour

    your corpse

I know my soul is small, it just wants a decent hotel room

& the man who lies down to sleep so trustingly beside me

to open his eyes & love me

IN THE AFTERLIFE,

if you were Greek, you might end up in Elysium, which was like Heaven
    only with better music
& also sports if you were tired of lounging in the shade of an olive tree

drinking a flinty Assyrtiko from Santorini or a Peloponnesian red, but then
    again Minos
might damn you to dreary Tartarus for murder or robbing a temple—
    slaughter & gold,

slaughter & many bronze statues. In my religion, which is basically who the
    fuck knows
what happens after we die & no one can prove anything anyway,

I imagine the spirits of some of those Greeks crawling into their marble
    likenesses
to hunker down inside the folds of a stone robe, looking out with their
    painted eyes

until the paint faded, losing their arms & noses, genitalia sheared off, their
    heads stolen,
torsos dazzling & instructing the lyric poets. When my mother was dying
    & couldn't speak

I sat with her & told her I knew she was in there, listening, & what might
    have been a tear
appeared on her worn old cheek, but really, I had no idea. All I could see
    was her suffering.

In Athens I saw bodiless pairs of feet, all that was left of whoever they
    were—even the gods
couldn't keep from disappearing, replaced by racks of cheap souvenir
    laurel crowns,

mati pendants & brightly decorated phallus keychains. The Greeks believed
the dead were kept alive by memory, but my religion says nothing brings
    them back

& you can't even touch the statues in museums. At the ruined Temple of
    Olympian Zeus
three wild parrots crossed the walkway in front of me, all in a row. Like a
    fallen

green & living column, I thought, & then thought, No.

ORACLE AT DELPHI

The virgin priestesses kept getting raped by the pilgrims
so later the job was filled by noblewomen of a certain age, prescient

& unfuckable, high on volcanic fumes
or maybe something in the water, but anyway

given to confusing interpretations of the word of Apollo because
who knew what went on inside the head of a god.

Inscrutability is 90 percent of divinity
or maybe it's more like the entire burrito of mystery meat

from that taqueria I suspected of conducting ritual animal sacrifice
out back where something was constantly burning & smelled bad.

Religion smells bad almost everywhere though originally
it might have been okay until the priests got hold of it.

A lot of goats died at Delphi. Historically, a lot of gods died
or got rebranded, then Jesus showed up & went viral & now

some people believe in trees, some in one-eyed demons, some
in nuclear superiority. The future is anyone's guess. O

ancient Pythias, Vedic astrologers, gifted psychics available online 24/7,
what does this hexagram on my forehead portend? Where

can I afford to live unmolested by rent raises, extreme weather events,
strangers at the door at three A.M. asking for someone named Veronica?

For here there is no veronica. Only me & my ineluctable shadow
holding aloft its Magic 8 Ball, searching for the weak Wi-Fi signal. In Delphi

the annoying tour guide, a proud Athenian, expressed her scorn for all
things not Greek as she led our group sweating up Parnassus in the sun.

She believed in her troubled country. Coming back down
we heard singing I might describe as angelic, if I believed in anything

as whack as angels. It was an old man in shredded trousers & a mariner's cap
with a face like a half-smashed tomato. He was playing a tzouras,

a small, six-stringed, plaintive instrument, & was soon harassed
from the roadside by three cops on motorcycles. Who can tell

his fate? Wherever he is, may he be adored
by the flowers at his bare & dirty feet.

SELF-PORTRAIT WITH A STATUE OF FERNANDO PESSOA

I could die any minute, so why not drink myself into cerebral hypoxia,

a state of impaired consciousness characterized by a marked diminution in
the capacity to react to environmental stimuli,

is one of those questions no one has yet answered to my satisfaction

Another is, since life is briefer than a squirrel orgasm, why don't I just go
to Lisbon

& stand beneath the statue of Pessoa that wears a book for a face until I
resemble it

which is another way of asking Why am I wasting my life sitting here
hating my hair

I could at least be lying in a hammock on someone's farm & writing

about butterflies & the golden shit of cows

But I don't really care about butterflies, especially when they land in poems

& I don't want to estheticize shit either

though I'm okay with Francis Bacon pointing to a pile of it & using it as a
metaphor for life

which is something I read once on a card in an exhibit of his paintings

Maybe "life is shit" is a good enough reason for starting in on the tequila
even without the unpromising coda
Añejo is waiting in the cupboard above the stove like a World War One recruit

about to be dragged out & thrown into a trench waiting for the guy next to him
    to die
so he can have his rifle, because there aren't enough rifles
In a war death may wear you for a face, & someone else can describe it

I mean if you're actually in it, not joysticking a drone, strung out on Jack &
    Red Bull
I mean if a mortar splashes onto your stove or the roof of your bus
I mean thinking about war makes me want to drink myself into a state of
    impaired etc.

Then again I've never been in a war so why am I being so morbid
Sometimes my brain takes a thick *Guernica*-colored Sharpie & scrawls all over
    the scenic view
& it helps to spill something with at least 11–14 percent alcohol on it

Pessoa was a pretty morbid person, often terrified & depressed

He wrote a poem about dying young, & he died at only forty-seven—of
alcoholism

"Only" means I'm older than he was when he died, sick & tired of almost
everything

Sometimes I just want to go someplace quiet enough to hear my bones
grinding together

Then again maybe the world isn't terrible & I just need a different leave-in
smoothing conditioner

A compact folding home treadmill to get me moving again

I shouldn't ask for so much from life

Even butterflies sometimes have to dine on urine & turtle tears & rotting
corpse ooze

while I've got a nice Sancerre with a hint of stony minerality chilling in
the fridge

Maybe I'll take a trip to Portugal & pour some on Pessoa's tomb

& when I die—did I mention it could be any minute—you could visit me

& remind me of how beautiful it all was

ACCORDING TO THE BUDDHISTS

that giant bottle of Patrón Silver on top of my fridge is already broken,
    even though it's still up there
& yes possibly not for long because it almost falls every time I take down
    the blender

Also, I'm already dead in spite of right now being propped up on pillows in
    bed between my two
presumably also already-deceased cats & it's true the one with cancer has
    been vomiting more lately

but why rush things into nonexistence . . . when life is already full of
    reminders
that we're all like that guy in the old silent film who climbs up the side of
    a building

& finds himself dangling from the minute hand of a big clock, the clock
    face slowly peeling away
He finally makes it safely onto the roof & kisses the girl & off they go arm
    in arm

which isn't the end of the story, because there they are gaily traipsing into
    1923
while the actor, Harold Lloyd, died in 1971, so he's definitely already dead

I think maybe I've got it backward, though, or just don't understand the point

I guess it's okay that everything gets broken, so we can just . . . relax . . . &
    meditate some more

on the void or a mental lotus blossom but I've never been able to meditate,
    mostly I drink
to feel calmer & stop thinking so much about death & impermanence

I'd like to be more sanguine about it all, I'd like to unscrew the lid on the
    jar of myself
& be okay that I'm already not breathing, but then I remember the bee

my friend & I once snagged from a swimming pool convinced it was from one
    of those killer swarms
& trapped in an empty olive jar, then watched as it crawled more & more
    slowly until it stopped

& I don't want to be that bee . . . I want to forget where things are headed . . .
I don't want my portrait to be a painting of rotting fruit & slaughtered birds

beside a caved-in scented candle, I want to be brush-stroked into the boating
    party luncheon
at that restaurant on the Seine, Maison Fournaise, I want the wine they're
    still having

According to the Buddhists, wanting is the cause of suffering so it's best to
    just . . . give up . . . & not mind . . .
Actually that bottle of tequila did finally crash down, & ended in big
    glittery shards

scattered all over the stone tiles, and—full confession—even the bee revived,
something to do with the brine in the jar, & we let it go to die another day

& I understand all this about as much as I understand the nature of time
which according to the physicists is not what's measured by clocks & doesn't
    even exist

at the teeniest, tiniest level, where there isn't any past or future or even a
    present moment
like this one, as you read this, to accept and be okay in, or . . . possibly . . .
    not.

THIS TOO SHALL PASS

was no consolation to the woman
whose husband was strung out on opioids.

Gone to a better place: useless and suspect intel
for the couple at their daughter's funeral

though there are better places to be
than a freezing church in February, standing

before a casket with a princess motif.
Some moments can't be eased

and it's no good offering clichés like stale
meat to a tiger with a taste for human suffering.

When I hear the word *miracle* I want to throw up
on a platter of deviled eggs. *Everything happens*

for a reason: more good tidings someone will try
to trepan your skull to insert. When fire

inhales your house, you don't care what the haiku says
about seeing the rising moon. You want

an avalanche to bury you. You want to lie down
under a slab of snow, dumb as a jarred

sideshow embryo. What a circus.
The tents dismantled, the train moving on,

always moving, starting slow and gaining speed,
taking you where you never wanted to go.

JUMP IN THE RIVER AND DROWN

Sometimes, actually, a terrible notion.
Stick around, a new season will soon drop

its episodes, little spores of narrative possibility
even if some characters were written off the show.

Sometimes crowds of black birds surge over the balcony,
proving the angelic hordes still occasionally

fling themselves earthward, but
sometimes a rock formation in the desert is just

a rock formation, even if it looks like a cathedral spire
or the penis of a stone god asleep underground.

Sometimes a liver's flopped out like a dead flounder
and replaced with one that blinks slowly,

pulsing through its colors until it matches
a medium-rare chunk of meat, as happened, luckily,

with my brother. Sometimes just before dusk
collapses over 26th and Broadway,

over God's Gym and the Volkswagen dealership,
I sit on my balcony to smoke a joint and watch the sky

scatter birds in all directions. My brother lived
a few more years, then disappeared

the way a sock does in the laundry. Where do they go?
What kind of terrible simile is that? He was my brother

but, say the creatures flapping by, he meant nothing
to us. Sometimes when I go to the desert I feel

the silence wants to tell me something and I stand
very still. Just to see if anything down there moves.

KANSAS, FOUR A.M.

The train brakes to take the bend behind the grain mill.

All night, at the motel, you listen to the ice machine's cold labor.
Does it ever stop?

Thunk. No, says the vending machine as the next train goes by.

On the highway the big rigs whine,
some carrying things that would kill you if one jackknifed off the overpass.

The chicken truck passes with its load of small-brained misery.

You can't hear the chickens, but you sort of think you can,
the way you can almost hear the sounds of the bar car on the train—

the bleary passengers trapped in their windows,

peering through their doppelgangers at the black
fields of wheat as they whiz past.

Childhood, did it ever exist?

What about the bar your father drank in, giving you
endless quarters for pinball . . . There it goes,

carried aloft by a maniacal wind.

Before science, a lot of wind gods
blew things around. The dead went to live on the moon.

A man might be half scorpion, a woman half fish.

An omniscient, omnipotent stranger who looked
like Santa Claus and had a throne in outer space

knew everything about you, yet still somehow loved you unreasonably.

Another chunk of ice clunks into the bin.
Under your window, an insect in the bushes scrapes out its longing.

The sounds of the world at this late hour sadden you,

but then enters the rain, hastening down, the rain that wants
to touch everything

and almost does.

BEATITUDE

Oh lord, I don't call anyone Lord.
I believe in the lower-case word,

the tiny multicolored lights strung
over the bar, blinking all year, the hunger

assuaged by peanuts & pork skins,
the benevolent screens of televisions

wavering benedictions
over the convivial, afflicted men,

the woman crowned with a knit hat,
all in the tempered pall of daylight—

dimlight, darklight, the lost & half-assed
more denizens than citizens who cast

their prayers high into sagging nets
tangled with lacy fish, blessed

by no one & buoyed
toward the heaven of the ceiling tiles.

BLUES ON AVENUE C

At night from my window I'd watch the liquor store owner

drag down his metal door, the spray-painted portrait

of his wife materializing above the dates of her birth

& death, she had those eyes that follow

you around, I couldn't see the stars that winter

unless they froze & fell like broken glass, the moon was so

high it looked like an overdose, I was so sick with grief

I wanted to stab a streetlight behind its curtain of fog & deliver

a mournful soliloquy to a trembling dog under

a blank marquee, the stoplights rocked in

ruthless wind, delivery bikes churned through the slushy intersection,

a staggering, blanket-clad couple paused to argue beneath

the wife's uneven blue eyes, their voices rising up to meet me

full of song & misery

COMPASSION PROBLEM

By season two of *The Walking Dead* I've almost grown immune

to corpses staggering along a road or through the woods drawn

by gunshots, bells, some music, like old dolls leaking

dust only blood spews out if you cut or stab or aim

a car through them, you might pull at one & its arm

comes off, their lips come off & show their teeth, you have to shoot

between their eyes or sink an axe into a skull to kill

the brain that's been someway hot-wired to start the whole

mess, the living are fewer & the undead more & more

legion, who'd want to see that on their way to get coffee, & so

ugly you want the former sheriff & his wife & son

& the old farmer & his daughters & the pizza guy & a few

others you've come to care about to solve those grotesque

cartoons, clear them from the streets & alleyways, & soon.

TRACES

The house falling down, the mantel broken off and moved to a corner.

The car in the garage, new in 1957, still looked new.

The man before he died had lived alone in a bedroom,

TV rolled out from the wall on a cart. He'd walked to the bathroom

so often he'd worn a path in the carpet, a detail that afterward

the real estate agent noted

as she'd noted the valuable car and the ruined mantel. Gone

except still there in her head years later, told at dinner

when she no longer remembered who or where

and no one thought to ask. Anyway, nothing's left. Maybe

a stone or child somewhere. Words over bread and too much wine.

Maybe a cautionary tale, maybe just another anecdote.

No bruise or burden, nothing to quicken the heart.

Something to vex the annihilating silence.

ANOTHER SPRING

Where are the fireworks by which I
can kneel once more before a man
and be humiliated by romantic expectations,
down the black air rivulets of light
dying on the surface of the Mediterranean?
What about those women at the gym today, dry
as old sandwiches, and as lonely . . .
waiting as if for the opera conductor in his dirty tuxedo.

The dogs on Rose Street are frantic—probably a coyote
has come down from the hills, hungry
for what raccoons left strewn by the bins.
At St. Gabriel's the bells bang and swing.
Next door a little boy has begun sobbing.
Where is the church of hands, the small doors opening . . .

BAD MOTEL

Isn't this a terrible motel? Aren't those people in the next room
fucking, what else, of course they are, slamming the bed
against the wall, & the toilet when we flush it roaring like a suckhole
swallow us down to Hell. Okay I love you. End of story.

Okay so we're just getting started. Air conditioner stuck
on freezing, kill it & here comes suffocation & throwing off the sheets.
Then that rotting narwhal corpse on the beach, gulls tugging out
the blubber, enormous picked-over spine dragged by the sea a few

yards away—the thing is, maybe I finally have to give up
falling on the rusty nails of affliction, combing through the trash
for the magic ring to make me disappear. Whoever said love
isn't pain didn't know what they were talking about but neither

did I when I said it's meant to fail & do you feel me through the sobbing
next door, listen to their tenderness now.

UPSTATE

Nature's a beautiful bitch.
Nightshade along the Hudson & in

an old stone house the floorboards
warp with nostalgia.

I have friends with hearts that stutter,
one going slowly blind.

Nature says *Love me*
or don't, I don't care.

Woods full of deer ticks & felled
trees from last year's ice storm.

Poppies emblazoning a field.
Bean-sized shadow on an X-ray.

Deep red, & flowering—
Slut. Slit. Opening

& blackening the day.

TIDAL

—for Donna

Rain comes back to the East River,
never the same river

but the buildings still toss their lights
on the water like flaming cocktails, the ferry

groans as it docks and then turns
away. Rain returns

to the river and goes
wherever souls go, thronging

forward and falling back. Your sister
at the end, flushed with morphine, called out

to the gone dog of your childhoods *Here*
girl, here—

Come in from the balcony, honey.
I've made you some food.

Sit in this chair and force it down
and we'll hate God together and remember her.

PARIS

After her fall Terrel got a new glass eye that when she wore it looked so perfect

you'd never guess it wasn't real but by the time it was made she preferred

to wear one of her patches, at first pirate black but then silver or glittery

gold, they suited her so well we all admired her and when the cancer

news hit her—I was about to say *blindsided* her, suddenly not a metaphor—

she fucked off to Paris with Porter for a vacation and that was so her,

we all agreed, the group of us who got together over dinner

every few weeks and there was always someone who someone knew or

heard of who'd died, or was nearly there, maybe just so old or in the hospital, our

custom during each story was to knock our wineglasses together and proclaim

    We're

alive! In the end—if that's an end—the cancer scare was just that, not so dire,

after all. Would you prefer the darkness—who knows what horror

will greet us next, like a concierge with a condescending stare—

or the lemon soufflé? Wherever we're going, we're already nearly there.

UNLEAVING

How long to grieve for the aspens, how long
for the father, half-paralyzed drugged up & pissing in
a plastic orange juice jug, & Christ, aren't you sick
of the endless mournful processional, the on & on song
of the ending of everyone, can we get on the dance floor
even if the music is tinny & wrong, & the mother took so long,
ten years of shuffling down a corridor, pushing a walker,
never mind, who cares, shut up, bong, bong, bong
go the church bells, *By my lively voice I drive away all harm*
was the inscription once, & in the fields the sheep
went along baaing & banging their bronze bells in old Rome
keeping the terrible spirits at bay, now go to sleep,
how long for the goddamned cat, what's wrong with you?
Just because it's night, and raining. Me too, me too.

SOLACE

for Terrance Hayes

Once when my coat
was too thin, and one torn
pocket was all I had left of
a great love, I found
a blue canto
that calmed me. A pine
tree was in it, and crows.
In my head: one ant
after another, carrying
its burden. Art
sometimes can enter
through a sliver.
Give it a broken fence, it
will trellis over. Once,
when no one was near,
a split tree
calmed me,
and a crow's cry tore
the air, and my ear
found an oar,
and I rowed.

NIGHT OUT

There are artists who don't want to have that conversation, she said

and I nodded but didn't know what she meant by that conversation.

Look at that amazing tree, I said. The waves crashed and flattened

almost before they had curled, the surfers were out,

we watched them from the road above, behind the *chiesa*.

Almost Easter. At dinner, a dessert case full of what it promised.

Another drink was a bad idea but some wanted it and it came to pass.

Another evening went up in mist. Went down in talk.

With her polka-dot gloves and wrong shoes. With his carefully insouciant
    scarf.

So much food! Were we being fattened for slaughter? Yes, in a manner

of thinking. Someone pointed out Mars and took a photo of the moon.

The train passed into the tunnel bored through the cliff, a sound I had
    come to love.

We can come to love. It's still possible, someone said, finishing their drink.

Then we all went to bed alone in the villa.

EXISTENTIAL ELEGY

Maybe everyone is walking around thinking something abstract and
  ontological
like *The existence of others as a freedom defines my situation*

and is even the condition of my own freedom. Maybe De Beauvoir
opens her notebook & writes it as soon as she sits down at the Deux Magots.

Life is inherently meaningless, probably thinks Sartre, across from her at the
  table,
studying the waiter. The chef savagely prepares a tart for its destruction.

Yet the street lamps blink on without thinking *Light, then nothing* . . .
as the booksellers along the Seine close their green boxes.

Humming, a woman pulls her damp dress from a basket,
then clothespins her simulacrum to the line.

So maybe not everyone. Maybe I can just lie here on the couch & pet the cat
the rest of the afternoon. He seems troubled

ever since the other one died. He won't chase that snaky rainbow thing
when I drag it over the carpet. What is he thinking? *Snaky rainbow things*

are but fleeting pleasures distracting us from the terror of the void that awaits us?
My first & only time in Paris was thirty years ago. It was February, &
    snowing.

I wandered Montparnasse cemetery while heady thoughts flurried
from the clouds, wet my face & disappeared. Everyone I loved was still alive.

Paris is still there. The *bouquinistes* too—rare editions & magazines,
    postcards, souvenirs.
The Deux Magots is still there. But now, supposedly, everyone interesting
    goes to the Flore.

Look at them, alive in this poem, holding their menus & about to disappear.
De Beauvoir weeps as Sartre's lowered in.

JAZZ IN 20/20

Sometimes you just need to hide in your room

and play all your old records backward.

The dissonant note resolves to a mellow tone.

The wooden boy resolves to become a real one,

but the real boy, crushed by the training wheels of academia,

only wants to stand in a forest, his leaves dripping with early fog,

blue nightingales on his forearms.

The gardenias in Billie Holiday's hair are no more.

People are improvising masks from their underwear.

The president is an obese virion.

It's hard to play anything with these waterlogged drumsticks,

hard to see the forest for the smoldering.

Ellis Marsalis and Wallace Roney are no more.

Bra cups are the right shape, but try breathing through one.

Try resolving to become more woke

while some corporate behemoth breaks out the cigars

and ashes all over your bicycle.

The long arc of the moral universe is no more.

The snow-blurred night in Greenwich Village with my brother

where we listened to the pianist at Mezzrow

play brilliantly for almost no one is no more.

What will survive of us is moot.

If you make a mistake, repeat it; that's what God did.

Sometimes you need to end where you began.

ESCHATOLOGY

No way this ends with everyone rising from the family plot
& rattling toward the celestial courthouse to be judged. Are we all
    frightened villagers?

Well, yes. Everyone's cowering from something. Right now, yet another
    atmospheric river
is dumping stalled container ships of rain on the house, uprooting trees on
    the hillside

& in the Christ-addled brain of my neighbor, the divine horses are being
    brushed & saddled,
angels are polishing their instruments, struggling into their armor. It's true

that things look more accurate, prediction-wise, if your prediction is more
    flooding & wildfires,
more monstrous bugs scuttling toward the corridors of power. My
    neighbor believes

she's pure enough to be resurrected & Hoovered into heaven while the
    secular infidels moan
about science & get trampled underfoot. If I have to think about resurrection,
    all I see

is a Netflix series where reanimated jake-legged corpses shuffle through
    the streets
while the real humans kill them again, & often each other, the
    compromised world

of the future pretty much already here. But how did we get into this
    discussion?
Someone brought up the Book of Revelation at the barbeque last week

over a few grilling chicken thighs. My neighbor, who thinks I'm the Whore
    of Babylon,
watched me disapprovingly as I refilled my wineglass of abominations

& spoke of God's people as credulous idiots. She said she would pray for me,
smug in the knowledge of my imminent destruction. Oh, to be that certain.

I almost admired her. But like the Whore of Babylon I was
I told the dirtiest joke I could think of, & watched her grow red-faced &
    offended,

& there the neighborly visit quickly ended.

DIVINATION

Everybody got the future wrong. We're still not flying between high-rises
    in our cars, zipping
past a hospital's fifth-floor window late at night where a sentient robot's
    squeegeeing clean

an operating room and listening to a podcast on writing, bitterly dreaming
    of literary fame.
No one believed we would one day fly to the moon, except in a song. Well,
    scientists did

and they were right so there goes my dumb thesis, sailing into the Weddell
    Sea,
sinking like a doomed Arctic expedition. Speaking of ice, someone
    predicted the resurrection

of a cryopreserved mouse by 2035 but that mouse probably won't be happy
    to find itself
still stuck in some lab, needle-poked by humans in white coats, which is
    one of the problems

with the future—it looks suspiciously like the past, another war to end all
    wars, another targeted ad
trying to sell you the spatula you bought last week. Try figuring out the future

by studying the cracked shoulder blade of a just-baked pig. Someone
     predicted that in a few
years we'll be starving, or else eating bugs which some people eat already
     and seem

to like but ugh, a friend once sent me fried ants from Brazil and I gagged
     just looking at them.
The world gets less palatable by the minute, and according to that lavishly
     bewigged polymath

Leibniz, God made the best of all possible worlds so this is as good as it
     gets, hallelujah, but
ugh, again. At seven, I thought I'd be a nun when I grew up. I tried to
     sacrifice

my beloved stuffed lion but when no angel came down to claim it, I lost my
     faith
and one day the dog ate my lion. In 2027 the asteroid 1999 AN10 will come

perilously close to earth. When this kind of thing happens in movies,
     there's usually a hero
or heroes, misfits and fuckups, who save the planet but it's not the planet
     that needs saving,

the earth will outlast it all at least until it's swallowed by the sun. Who and
　　what we were
will be recorded on a strand of DNA embedded in a plastic bunny blasted
　　into space to travel

who-knows-where and be found, or not, by who-knows-what. That's my
　　prediction,
which came to me in a dream just last night after I twisted for hours in
　　the sheets,

insomniac and sweating and miserable.　In the dream I was that bunny,
and lonely.

SELF-PORTRAIT WITH HEAVY RAIN

Another day of lying face-down,

trying to transubstantiate some fucked-up feeling into a certified ethical

   diamond.

Another day staring out the window at the trees . . .

Today they look thin & helpless, like my dying mother hauled from bed,

made taller & multiplied.

A squirrel runs across her blouse, down her stained sweatpants, & disappears.

Heavy rain falling like gray squirrels,

like drool from the mouth of a goddess in an unbuttoned sweater,

like Restylane filling in the potholes, making the world look attractively

   prehistoric.

The sky's flushed its medication down the toilet.

Power lines arc, a telephone pole heaves itself through a car roof.

The driver's flattened, but not her baby in the backward-facing seat.

I wonder if that's the act of a merciful or a monstrous god.

Maybe bipolar is the word I'm looking for,

but no one wants to be defined by their illness,

not even my mother,

being crushed like a hunk of coal to be loaded into a barge

& towed downriver . . .

Maybe a comforting angel is inching along the electromagnetic spectrum
     looking for me,

just not very hard,

the way I looked for jobs when I was on Unemployment.

Another day incentivizing dust mites, waiting for bad news . . .

Earthworms curled up in the dark, waiting to surface from their drenched
     burrows

& shrivel on sidewalks in the sun.

CRACKED LOGIC

There's a crack in everything, that's how the light gets in. —Leonard Cohen

Yes, but Pandora cracked open the jar lid & look what happened.
Kilauea cracked open & out came molten rock,
creeping through the subdivisions, oozing into the ocean.

From fracking, methane. Ditto from pig shit & cow farts.
The worms get in, the worms get out . . .

Crack a cow & out come hamburgers, fatty steaks, cancer & heart disease.
Coconuts: nearly impossible to crack open, so best to find one
already halved, filled with a blended pina colada & a straw.

Out of the beginning of time creeps the end.
Out of the fetal monitor, the ICU ventilator.

Yes, but out of the cradle came Whitman, after many prepositional phrases,
to sing about listening to a bird,
& once I watched baby rabbits pour from a hole in our backyard

so that was a lot of light getting out.

A crack is a tear is a hole is a gap.
A rat is a pig is a dog is a boy.

The fourth wall of this poem has a crack in it.
Hello, pilgrim. Welcome to my labyrinth.

You're not the only one who's losing the thread, this far in.
The glittering thread.

But let's keep going.
This is all that's keeping me from drinking myself shitfaced.

The Liberty Bell: cracked & recast, cracked again & now mute.
When you crack an egg in a broken country, bits of shell may float away
like lifeboats for tiny refugees fleeing over the cracked lithosphere.

The heart doesn't crack, even when dropped from a great height,
though it may feel as though shattering has occurred.

You probably know exactly what I mean.
If you don't, you are likely a reanimated corpse
or Mitch McConnell.

When ancient Egyptians were mummified, their viscera were stored in
     canopic jars,
because who couldn't use a liver or stomach in the afterlife,

but the heart was left where it was, beneath the rib cage, intact.
When my mother was no more,

When my mother was cremulated,
When my mother,

When—

I saved some of her in a tiny jam jar.
It smelled like raspberries.

VANISHING POINT

Is it just me, or is this painting upside down? I can't tell an altar from a
    urinal.
Apparently, art is not to be trusted. It keeps hiding the walls

when you just want something to lean your forehead against and weep to.
This road only looks like it leads somewhere.

In Van Gogh's painting "The Café Terrace at Night"–starlight, lamplight,
a few empty tables—the focal point is the waiter in white,

who can't see you standing there, thirsty and sad, a few feet away.
Here's a dead father's handkerchief, its corners embroidered with flowers.

Here are men in bowler hats, floating stolidly in mid-air. A word where a
    sob should be.
A reluctant heifer dragged toward slaughter around and around on an urn.

Sure, it won't ever be butchered but how would you like to find yourself
trapped in that scene for eternity? After a while you just want to give up

and say, *Kill me now.* There are feelings no mocktail can cure. Here's the
    photo
that proves someone once loved you, just not for long.

Here in the ruins, an ancient stone statue of a woman, missing her arms
and her mother. Meanwhile, back at the museum, a basketball floats

in the center of an aquarium, not sinking but not rising either.
Let's go get a real drink before we succumb to whatever's going to
    destroy us.

Meanwhile, someone is walking away down the railroad tracks in this poem
never to be heard from again.

THEREFORE I AM NOTHING

It's probably best not to think too much about my terminally ill cat
or to wonder whether my mentally ill brother is dead or alive right now
which makes me think of my cat again because of Schrödinger's
    experiment—

what was it anyway—some kind of thought experiment
I remember there was a cat in a box & some poison
But I don't want to think about poison, another bad thing in my head

except that now I am, but at least I don't personally know anyone who was
    poisoned—
ancient kings & nobles, Hercules & hatters, some enemies of Putin—
so I'm feeling okay now, *poison poison poison*, no anxiety at all

People are waiting in line in Mexico to fill tanks with oxygen for dying
    abuelas
The Greenland ice sheet is melting faster than a butter stick in a microwave
Australian clownfish can't find the reef, all that noise from humans & their
    machines

That's how I think of it, *humans & their machines,* like I'm not one of them
But I am & now I have to bring up Descartes
who thought animals had no minds, just mechanical sensations

One more anthropocentrist ruining the picnic for everyone

Can't we all just take off our helmets & be nectar in a bee-loud glade

Open the box, don't open the box, ignore the box, the cat knows

Also I don't understand Cartesian dualism but I hate it

with a simplistic, uncomprehending hatred

unlike the jaded & cosmopolitan disgust I feel for God

I guess the cat can't know anything if it's already dead

& something went wrong with my brother's brain years ago

& if the earth is having any thoughts, they're probably along the lines of

    Stop poisoning me

Now I'm wondering whose ashes were scraped from the columbarium

    along with my mother's

I don't think she's playing tennis with Jesus in heaven

Mostly I try not to think at all anymore

just stare at the place between words & their meanings

& wait for some less monstrous feeling to be born

& stumble toward me

PREDATOR REPORT

In Siberia, the man whose future is to be dismembered by a vengeful
   Amur tiger
patrols the forest and tends his beehives, eking out survival in a land

no one in their right mind wants to visit, except maybe poachers.
When my cat licks itself, I imagine a tiger stripping fur and meat from a
   carcass

with its tongue. A wild tiger's carcass can be stripped for parts and sold
   illegally to China
for ancient and dubious medical cures. Baldness, epilepsy, insomnia. Is
   there a cure

for the feeling that life is one long accommodation to loss, and if so,
is there something I can kill to get it? I am here to report

that one way or another, everything gets torn apart.
I keep my cat inside so it won't dine on the resident avians or be devoured

by coyotes. Some nights, a pack of them trots down the fire road
to kill some smaller creature beyond the chain link.

You get used to the sounds. You close the window

and go back to sleep. Another species goes extinct.

And life gets smaller while the cries fall, as Brecht wrote,

like rain in summer, though he was referring not to animals

but to humans, and I am here to further report that lately,

even the rain has started acting strange.

I BELIEVE THIS WAY OF LIFE IS ENDING, I SAID

to Elizabeth & we will look back amazed

at water at backyards & supermarkets I bought

cheeses & flatbread we were eating as

I talked drinking good wine Chad had chosen

for us imagine wine imagine choosing how amazing

it was all going to be as we stood in line with our cancers

& bowls while small mechanical birds whizzed

around us keeping an eye on things i.e. us & violence

tore a few people open as usual though now of

course more & more so it was getting hard to

see much given how many shreds of

how many souls were snowing down getting

crushed underfoot they used to make wine that

way imagine I said amazing & we raised

our glasses again the taste rippling down our throats

like flags or rolls of crepe or maybe toilet paper

tossed into a surviving tree after rain & still clinging there.

JOURNEY TO THE END OF SEASON ONE OF
AMERICAN HORROR STORY

The night the season ended I dreamed there was a new viral trend, it went
   like this
First you were doused with a bucket of freezing water
then bisected from the top of your head down through your groin with a
   very sharp sword

It was supposed to happen quickly, like a glass fiber-optic internet download
& when it was over you were still alive

In the dream I had somehow agreed to try it, why not, take a risk, have an
   adventure
The water was so cold my pee immediately froze in my bladder, & I thought
   Should I tip the swordsman?
like I was Anne Boleyn, about to be *décapitée,* & then he stepped toward me

In *Journey to the End of Night* Louis-Ferdinand Céline wrote about surviving
   in a brutal world
saying *You can be a virgin in horror the same as in sex*

I had decided to watch *American Horror Story* at the urging of my friend

Well maybe not urging but he'd mentioned it had a lot of seasons

& I liked bingeing shows on my treadmill rather than actually going
outside for a walk in the city

My Citizen app was constantly showing me what was going on around me

Two-Encampment Fire .5 mi

Multiple Gunshots Heard .3 mi

Woman Assaulted with Saw 900 ft

Person Robbed .8 mi

Person Assaulted with Vehicle .2 mi

Robbery at Gunpoint 1200 ft

Citizen also kept me up to date with the latest Covid reports

The new variant was spreading like an oil slick over the unvaccinated,

their arm hairs matting and separating, their wings weighed down & filthy

A lot of things happened in Season One that required one actor to
dramatically put her hand to her face or chest

& another to act like things were pretty normal even when she was eating a
raw brain

& a third to give psychotherapy to a school shooter without reporting him

The trigger warnings at the start of the episodes went like this

gore, suicide, sex, smoking, nudity, violence, language

For anyone who's a virgin in horror you might need a few more

The house in the series, Murder House, true to its name, kept killing people

or the ghosts in the house kept killing people

or the guy who'd set fire to his family & burned half his face off kept killing
people

then hacking them into pieces to be buried under the gazebo or found by
the police

in "the colored section" of town, as Actor #1 put it, getting the news about
her boyfriend

(hand to chest, then face)

Her daughter kept sneaking into Murder House telling people *You're going
to die in here*

until she was killed by a hit-and-run driver on Halloween

The daughter who lived in the house killed herself but didn't realize she
was dead

until she found her own body folded into a crawl space, covered with
blowflies

I aimed for 7,000 steps a day on my treadmill

because a *New York Times* article said the recommended 10,000 was overkill

I was also trying IF, or intermittent fasting, which several readers in the
comments section

suggested would make for a longer life, a leaner body & sharper mind

& possibly also help my cholesterol levels

so I was watching everything on an empty stomach

The final episodes went something like this

The husband in the house is killed by other ghosts & found hanging from a
    chandelier

The school shooter (also dead) who's in love with the daughter gets his
    dead heart broken

The dead gay male couple decorates a bedroom as a nursery, walls & crib
    painted red

The ghost of the abortionist doctor delivers twins

At the end there's a touching Christmas moment, several of the deceased
    around a lit-up tree

Cut to the twin who wasn't stillborn, toddler Antichrist in a rocking chair,
    smiling

after murdering his nanny

So far there are ten seasons & number eleven is on its way

The second season is *American Horror Story: Asylum*

I'm wondering if I can stomach it & if not, what I should watch next

Everything interesting happens in the dark, Céline wrote

& I keep thinking *Does it? Does it?*

I feel like it's all out there already on display, & it goes like this

ODE TO ENGLAND

I love your cheeky TV bakers baking biscuit sheep & dragons
& lurid lemon tartlettes, drizzle cakes & sausage plaits—

I love your scandal docudramas, & how the violence of your crime shows
occurs mostly off-camera between cups of tea & the relentless

parsing of personal relationships, while here in America
the trope of the car chase has been replaced by the trope

of exploding heads. I like having a lie-in & watching onscreen your royal
families imploding in their castles & palaces, your late-blooming lovers

from different social classes arguing in pubs. Brilliant are your pubs &
    publicans,
your Thames & Tyne, your River Ouse that tried & failed to scour Virginia
    Woolf's voices

from her head—*If anybody could have saved me, it would have been you*, she
    wrote
to Leonard in heartbreaking conditionals—Even now, when I think of her,
    I want someone

to rescue her & offer to put on the kettle while she takes off those wet

    things—

You gave us so many things, England, macadam & matches, the flask & the

    light bulb

even before Edison, you gave Europe the Halifax gibbet five hundred

    years before

the guillotine—Maybe I shouldn't thank you for that—You gave us the

    gentleman's

cummerbund, useful for catching crumbs, slimming to the waist, though

    it originated

in your military when you were mucking about in India where you never

    belonged—

I probably shouldn't bring that up either—but I love the sound of

    cummerbund,

that elegant dactyl reminds me of other elegant dactyls, oh Benedict

    Cumberbatch—

half a league, half a league, half a league onward

& there are your soldiers again, doing & dying for someone's blunder

& there are the unmarked graves of the Kikuyu in Kenya—

Oh you're flawed, Britannia, the history of your rule as cruel as every other country, you're as terrible as America

& as beautiful, our connection is historical

& biological, too, 28 percent of me is you, I can follow my finger

back up the ancestral line to Edward I who was a shit to the Scots—

Bloody hell, I wanted a purer praise song but this is all I've got—

Meet me at the Mayflower Pub, by the river in Rotherhithe—

A toast to all our frailty

& the mess we make of everything eventually, but tonight

we'll raise a pint & exit singing loudly to the cobblestone street

& later we'll drink endless cups of tea.

TRANSFER OF POWER

Am I a purveyor of damage? Am I hurting you because I speak?
Are these knives in my hands? Very tiny ones? Slivers of glass?
Flesh is the glass. And the grass, what is it . . . and the dirt, who are they . . .
I don't know what I'm saying. Shut me up. I'm probably mad.
These are the ravings of all people in all times.

I watch the news shows every night. I'm tired of being ginned up.
I drink all day and listen to the flag ripping in the wind.
Somewhere my breech doppelganger is feeling the same way.
We want to kill each other. We have a purpose, now.
At last we are the battle. At last we are joined.

OHIO

Who am I to say that the hawk circling above the deck

wasn't really the murdered sister of our host,

as she insisted? Who says the dead stay dead, anyway

or even human—for all I know our souls stream out and leap

into the nearest form, manzanita, termite,

light pole, to begin the challenges of figuring out

when to break into blossom, how to find a mate

or glow softly each evening

without a single glass of wine. Our host

was downing grape juice and growing wild-eyed

about the government, unable to stop reliving

that day on the Kent State Commons over fifty years ago

when the Guardsmen turned in unison and fired on the students.

She was right about politics and false narratives

but wrong about the winged creatures swarming

from the eaves as we talked. Those weren't moths

but they were sort of lovely until we realized

they were busy eating her guest house

on the California coast, in the pleasant weather we were enjoying

thanks to the drought, grateful that smoke from the wildfires

had drifted elsewhere. As she kept on

I felt sympathy leak out of me until all I could think of

was how to be alone with my lover

and forget about my country's many crimes,

one of which was killing a college girl. Who, why not,

might have been coasting the thermals all day

looking to survive by killing something else. Who am I to say

a word. It's not my story. My love and I excused ourselves

and went inside to make dinner. In the nearby cove the breaking waves

endlessly bashed themselves against the rocks.

THE DISTANCE

The ATV crosses the wide, shallow river.

On one side, tin-roofed shacks. On the other, the air-conditioned tourist
hotel.

On one side of the woods, grandmother's cottage. On the other, you with
your little basket.

Always a gap between the platform and the train.

On one side, a pious wife in Avignon. On the other, many sonnets.

In one story, a transforming kiss. In another, drunken blow job in a
bathroom stall.

The bridal dresses stiffen in the window.

The flatworms unsheathe their two-headed swords.

The missile hisses down toward its target.

In the mud, scattered puddles of blood and rain.

To the right of the road, unexploded mines.

To the left, unexploded mines.

The luthier, weary, strings another violin.

Lorca sets out for Córdoba on his black pony, never to arrive or return.

DARK AND GETTING DARKER

Everyone needs a genie and a lamp.

Ancient red handprints in a hard-to-get-to cave.

A wireless charger for their liver

after years of heedless drinking.

Also, not to dematerialize before seeing Venice

which itself may soon dematerialize

beneath the Adriatic. Upstairs, my brother

bangs the supper dishes. My wish

is to be too drunk to think

about the sermon at the funeral mass today,

the priest mumbling no one knew what,

then the coffin fed into the back of the hearse

and driven off with another brother's body

while his widow went to pieces on the curb.

According to the internet, there are three things

a genie can't do: no granting the wish

for more wishes. No bringing back the dead.

Also, no making someone fall in love with you.

Luckily there are potions for that,

even if they're bad for your digestion. I wish

my friend had never been diagnosed with Parkinson's.

That we still lived together in that house

among the trees. I'd like to go there now

on a magically self-cleaning carpet

for when my dying cat throws up again,

and grieve.

ARIA DI SORBETTO

Welcome to the abattoir.

The opera is ending soon.

Get a taste of this raspberry tart

before the bad odor starts.

We'll all get our ears pierced, then burst into tears.

I just want to take off this fucking bra

and stare dumbly at the shining Mediterranean.

Don wants to come back as a whale, but careful

what you wish for: you might find yourself entangled

in old fishing gear, strangled by a crab trap,

dragging your enormous, exhausted heart for years

until you succumb. Sort of like the human you already are.

Missing the gelato in that little Italian village.

Ah, ah, opera! It sounds like a whale that swallowed a musical

and I loathe musicals. But that time Josh suddenly

broke into song in the Eighth Avenue subway

beside the bronze Otterness sculptures—the workers

and politicians, the alligator swallowing a businessman

whose head is a moneybag—a thin shiv of joy

slipped under my ribs, and my daughter

took my hand as the train shrieked in and if you ask

me to love this world yes, oh yes,

I will.

BY WAY OF A REMINDER

Even though most of your family is underground
and your shield is made of cardboard and the backyard
is on fire again, it's best to ignore the sirens
inviting you to join them and instead
befriend an out-of-tune banjo, a broken
swing set, a grounded bee you can nurse
with sugar water or a trip to a sunflower.
The many synonyms for dark, they have
found me also; I assure you, even the leftovers
in the fridge have regarded me with suspicion.
Which of us is to be eaten next?—not a question
to ask a marauding tiger or incel with a bump stock
but to be fair, any question at all is probably
a bad idea in the moment, when it's best
to find the nearest wormhole. Mostly
you just need to keep walking deeper
into the desert, breaking your spear on rocks,
inscribing a few verses on whatever water
you can find, even if it's full of bark scorpions
breathing through their exoskeletons.
Mostly you need a night out, a new coat,
a provider who doesn't drop the call
in the middle of a sob. Maybe some good weed.

After that, it's up to the gods

who can't exactly be counted on

if history is any predictor, but that's no reason

to lose heart; look, a stray cat has found the recycling

bin of empty tuna cans outside on the porch

and wants in.

Acknowledgments

Gratitude to the editors of the following publications, where many of these poems first appeared:

Adroit Journal, *Alaska Quarterly Review*, *Ambit* (UK), *The Atlantic*, *Bath Magg* (UK), *Blackbird*, *Fiddlehead* (Canada), *Five Points*, *Frontier Poetry*, *James Dickey Review*, *Jung Journal*, *Live Encounters*, *The Nation*, *New England Review*, *The New Yorker*, *Pedestal*, *The Poetry Review* (UK), *Smartish Pace*, *The Southern Review*, *The Threepenny Review*, *The Yale Review*.

"Blues on Avenue C" appeared in the anthology *From the Inside: NYC from the Eyes of the Poets Who Live Here*, edited by George Wallace, from Blue Light Press (2022).

"Existential Elegy" from *New England Review* was selected by Mary Jo Salter for *Best American Poetry 2024* (Scribner).

"Exit Opera" was commissioned and performed for BBC Radio 3's *Between the Ears* for the show "California Burning," which I presented in September 2022. Thanks to my producer, Sara Jane Hall, for conjuring our far-flung adventures over the years.

"My Opera" appeared as Poem-of-the-Week in *Narrative*.

"This Too Shall Pass" appeared in Poem-A-Day from the Academy of American Poets.

I also wish to thank the Bogliasco Foundation for the support of a Bogliasco Foundation Fellowship that sparked the writing of several of these poems, and Van Cleef & Arpels for a creative fellowship. Thanks to La Romita School of Art for continued inspiration.

To my students, past and present: Thank you for being passionate about poems and sharing your imaginations and visions with me.

To my friends and family: Truly, madly, deeply.